W9-AZG-452

SPOTLIGHT ON SOCIAL AND EMOTIONAL LEARNING

HARD WORK AND DETERMINATION

DEVELOPING SELF-DISCIPLINE

RACHAEL MORLOCK

PowerKiDS press.

NEW YORK

Published in 2020 by The Rosen Publishing Group, Inc.
29 East 21st Street, New York, NY 10010

Editor: Rachel Gintner
Designer: Michael Flynn

Photo Credits: Cover Kevin Dodge/Blend Images/Getty Images; cover, pp. 1, 3–4, 6, 8, 10–14, 16–20, 22–24 (background) TairA/Shutterstock.com; p. 5 antoniodiaz/Shutterstock.com; p. 7 Sergey Novikov/Shutterstock.com; p. 9 Syda Productions/Shutterstock.com; p. 11 MikeDotta/Shutterstock.com; p. 11 Getty Images; p. 12 Bill Johnson/Denver Post/Getty Images; p. 13 Tom Williams/CQ-Roll Call Group/Getty Images; p. 15 VALERIE MACON/AFP/Getty Images; p. 17 Chris Ryan/Caiaimage/Getty Images; p. 18 Randy Faris/Corbis/Getty Images; p. 19 Diego Cervo/Shutterstock.com; p. 21 Iakov Fillmonov/Shutterstock.com; p. 22 Lapina/Shutterstock.com.

Cataloging-in-Publication Data

Names: Morlock, Rachael.
Title: Hard work and determination: developing self-discipline / Rachael Morlock.
Description: New York : PowerKids Press, 2020. | Series: Spotlight on social and emotional learning | Includes glossary and index.
Identifiers: ISBN 9781725302037 (pbk.) | ISBN 9781725302228 (library bound) | ISBN 9781725302136 (6pack)
Subjects: LCSH: Self-control--Juvenile literature. | Self-control in children--Juvenile literature. | Children--Conduct of life--Juvenile literature.
Classification: LCC BF723.S25 M67 2020 | DDC 179'.9--dc23

Manufactured in the United States of America

CPSIA Compliance Information: Batch #CSPK19. For further information contact Rosen Publishing, New York, New York at 1-800-237-9932.

CONTENTS

CHAPTER ONE

THE KEY TO SUCCESS

What's the difference between a beginner and a master, or between a great idea and a finished project? Usually, the answer lies in hard work, practice, and **dedication**. All three elements are a part of self-discipline.

Self-discipline is the inner strength that helps you be more healthy, productive, and successful in your life. It allows you to put aside something you want in the moment while you work for something you want in the future. Self-discipline also helps you stick to paths and habits that bring you closer to your goals.

The hope of reaching a goal fuels your self-discipline. If your goal is to have a strong body, self-discipline keeps you on track with healthy eating and exercise. Self-discipline comes from within you, so it works best when your goal is important and meaningful to you.

If you're aiming for good grades, you'll use self-discipline to do your homework and study for tests.

CHAPTER TWO

THE POWER OF SELF-DISCIPLINE

You might recognize words such as "willpower" and "self-control," which are related to self-discipline. A **psychologist** named Walter Mischel created what's called "the marshmallow test" for studying self-control. In each test, a preschooler was given a marshmallow and the choice to eat it right away or wait. If they waited, they could have an extra marshmallow. Could the children control their desire for the first marshmallow in order to have two marshmallows later?

This study continued as the preschoolers grew up. The children who used self-control in the experiment were more successful later as teenagers. Their grades and test scores were better than those of the children who hadn't waited for the second marshmallow.

Other studies show that self-discipline is more powerful than intelligence in school. Being hardworking and self-disciplined are the most important qualities in excellent students, and everyone can get better at self-discipline!

Resisting a reward that's available now in order to wait for a greater reward later is called "delayed gratification." In the marshmallow test, the reward was an extra marshmallow!

CHAPTER THREE

LOOKING FORWARD

Practicing self-discipline is **difficult**. It requires you to control your emotions, desires, and actions. It often involves following through on tough decisions, which can make using self-discipline uncomfortable at first. Think about the preschoolers' experience in the marshmallow test. Many children squirmed in their seats or tried to ignore the treat in front of them. They had to deal with the discomfort of waiting in order to earn their reward.

Self-discipline is geared toward the future. You have to think about your goal, even when you could have a pleasant experience in the present. Luckily, self-discipline gets easier with practice. As you build good habits, you don't have to struggle as much against the **temptations** of the moment. Creating a **routine** can take away some of your discomfort. Then, with every success, you can see the benefits of your self-discipline.

Procrastination gets in the way of self-discipline and can **distract** you from important tasks. Procrastination is putting off something that you have to do, such as homework.

CHAPTER FOUR

STRONG ATHLETES

Self-discipline is very important for success in school, but it plays a role, or part, outside the classroom as well. No matter the goal you're going after, self-discipline can help you get there. If your goals are related to sports, then self-discipline is fundamental.

Athletes use self-discipline to build strong bodies and master skills. They're **motivated** by a desire to win and perform well. Self-discipline guides their commitment to healthy eating, training their bodies, and practicing. It can take years and years to become a top athlete. Athletes show both self-discipline and grit, or mental strength, when they work very hard over a long period of time in order to reach a goal.

The Olympic runner Jesse Owens once said, "We all have dreams. In order to make dreams come into reality, it takes an awful lot of **determination**, dedication, self-discipline, and effort."

You can practice self-discipline in sports, too. You can choose **nutritious** foods, build your muscles with exercise, and test your skills. Self-discipline allows you to create healthy habits and stick to your athletic goals.

EXCEPTIONAL ARTISTS

What do good painters, musicians, writers, and other artists have in common? They all use self-discipline to perfect their craft. Learning artistic **techniques** takes practice, and artists must commit their time and energy to creating art.

Yo-Yo Ma began playing the cello at age four. He was six when this photo was taken while he performed with his sister. Today, Yo-Yo Ma is a world-famous musician.

YO-YO MA

Some successful artists have spent a lifetime building their skills, but it's never too early or too late to learn a new art form. Self-discipline can help you strengthen your abilities at any age. Consistency is also important for artistic **development**. You are consistent when you regularly behave a certain way. For most artists, steady, daily practice is the key to success.

Talent is important in art, but self-discipline and consistency are also necessary. You can become a self-disciplined artist by thoughtfully making time for your craft. Try saving a part of each day for playing a musical instrument, creating artwork, or writing in a journal.

CHAPTER SIX

ABOVE AND BEYOND

The benefits of self-discipline go beyond school, sports, and art. Self-discipline can help you with something as simple as making your bed every morning or as extraordinary as starting your own business.

There are many opportunities to use self-discipline throughout the day. You can follow a routine that helps you prepare for school in the morning. Another routine might guide you through nighttime tasks before bed. Do you have chores to do at home? When you actively plan and work to finish your chores, you practice self-discipline.

Practicing self-discipline with small tasks prepares you for times when you need a lot of self-discipline to reach your goals. Imagine that you have a self-discipline muscle. When you exercise that muscle, it gets stronger! With greater self-discipline, you can use your abilities and talents to go above and beyond the ordinary.

When she was in the fifth grade, Marley Dias created #1000BlackGirlBooks to bring stories about strong black girls to schools and libraries. She used self-discipline to start a movement while balancing her tasks at school and at home.

CHAPTER SEVEN

BUILDING SELF-DISCIPLINE

Other social and emotional skills, such as self-awareness, can help you build self-discipline. An important part of controlling your thoughts, feelings, and actions is noticing them. You can learn to pay attention and identify your emotions and experiences. If you're aware of thoughts or feelings that block self-discipline, then it's easier to decide how to deal with them. You can slow down and choose the best way to act in order to reach your goals.

You won't always succeed, but you can always improve. Making mistakes gives you an opportunity to look closely at your goals, actions, and emotions. This is a good time to reflect—what can you do to be more self-disciplined in the future? When you see the positive results of your self-discipline, you'll feel more assured that you can succeed again. Your hard work is paying off!

Reaching your goals through self-discipline can give you the push you need to set new and bigger goals for yourself.

SETTING GOALS

The secret to self-discipline is setting goals that mean something to you. The more you want something, the easier it is to work hard for it. Can you think of something you want to do or achieve? Maybe you'd like to win a writing contest, earn a science fair ribbon, or go to the Olympics. It's OK to have big dreams! No matter how large your dreams are, you can start by setting small goals.

When setting a goal, decide what you need to do and when you will do it. Advice from trusted adults can help you create a solid plan.

Begin by breaking down large goals into simpler tasks. Then, you can work through them one by one. Measuring and recording your progress might encourage you to stick with your goals. Charts, calendars, and checklists can help you track how far you've come and point to your next step. It's also smart to share your goals. Friends and family can offer ideas and support you along the way.

CHAPTER NINE

PLANNING AHEAD

You can set yourself up for success by planning ahead. Think about the distractions and temptations that might spoil your self-discipline. Then, change your surroundings so that it's easier to follow your plan. If you know your phone distracts you, leave it in another room while you practice an instrument. If you're trying to eat well, prepare a healthy snack in advance so that it's ready when you're hungry.

Another way to improve your focus is to stick to a clear and preplanned schedule. Tell yourself that you'll spend 30 minutes doing your homework as soon as you get home from school. If you make your decision beforehand, you can get right to work when the time comes. You can also **prioritize** your tasks if you have a lot to do. Plan to tackle the most important or difficult jobs first.

Martial arts can build self-discipline by teaching you to focus your attention and control your body. As you master skills, you work toward the goal of earning a new belt.

CHAPTER TEN

THE ROAD TO ACHIEVEMENT

As you practice self-discipline, it'll become easier to use in your daily life. Self-discipline runs on energy from your brain and body. You can fuel your body by getting enough sleep and eating nutritious foods. Focus on one task at a time and take a break between activities to recharge. Taking care of your body's needs will prepare you for times when self-discipline is necessary.

It's natural to make mistakes as you work toward a goal. When it's difficult to stay focused, try to remember the reasons behind your actions. You can remind yourself of your goal and its importance to you by drawing or writing about it. Once you've learned how to use it, self-discipline is powerful enough to change your life and turn your dreams into reality. With strong self-discipline and motivation, you can achieve your goals.

GLOSSARY

athlete (ATH-leet) A person who takes part in bodily exercise or sports.

dedication (deh-duh-KAY-shuhn) The act of working hard for a cause.

determination (duh-tuhr-muh-NAY-shuhn) The act of deciding definitely and firmly.

development (duh-VEHL-uhp-muhnt) The act or process of growing or causing something to grow.

difficult (DIH-fuh-kuhlt) Hard to do, make, or carry out.

distract (duh-STRAKT) To draw away attention.

martial art (MAR-shuhl AHRT) A type of self-defense or fighting that's practiced as a sport.

motivate (MOH-tuh-vayt) To provide with a reason for doing something.

nutritious (noo-TRISH-uhs) Containing things needed to grow and stay alive.

prioritize (pry-OHR-uh-tiyz) To list or rate in order of importance.

psychologist (sy-KAH-luh-jist) A person who studies psychology, or the science or study of the mind and behavior.

routine (roo-TEEN) A regular way of doing things in a particular order.

technique (tehk-NEEK) A method of accomplishing a task.

temptation (temp-TAY-shuhn) Something that tempts you or is appealing.

INDEX

PRIMARY SOURCE LIST

Page 11
Jesse Owens, U.S. Olympian, at the 1936 Summer Olympic Games. Photograph. January 1, 1936. Berlin, Germany. Getty Images Sport.

Page 12
Marie-Therese Yeou-Cheng Ma and Ernest Yo-Yo Ma. Photograph. Bill Johnson. December 16, 1961. Denver, Colorado. *Denver Post*.

Page 15
Marley Dias at the United State of Women Summit. Photograph. Valerie Macon. May 5, 2018. Los Angeles, California. AFP and Getty Images.

WEBSITES

Due to the changing nature of Internet links, PowerKids Press has developed an online list of websites related to the subject of this book. This site is updated regularly. Please use this link to access the list: www.powerkidslinks.com/SSEL/hardwork